FOREWORD

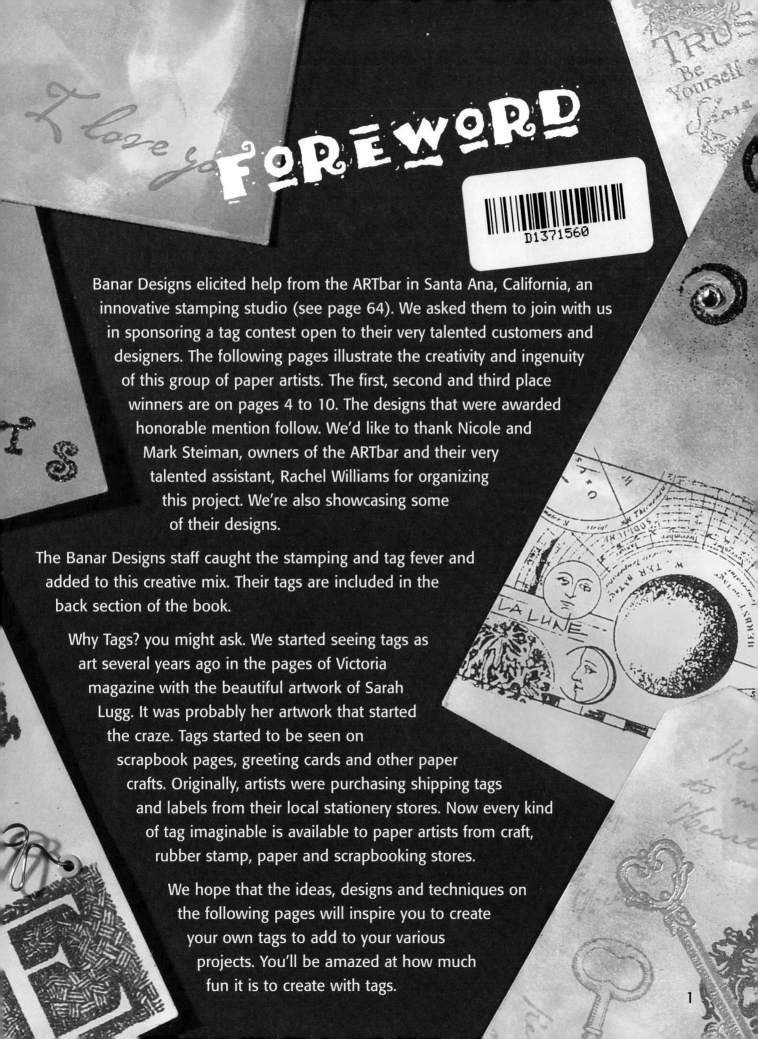

Banar Designs elicited help from the ARTbar in Santa Ana, California, an innovative stamping studio (see page 64). We asked them to join with us in sponsoring a tag contest open to their very talented customers and designers. The following pages illustrate the creativity and ingenuity of this group of paper artists. The first, second and third place winners are on pages 4 to 10. The designs that were awarded honorable mention follow. We'd like to thank Nicole and Mark Steiman, owners of the ARTbar and their very talented assistant, Rachel Williams for organizing this project. We're also showcasing some of their designs.

The Banar Designs staff caught the stamping and tag fever and added to this creative mix. Their tags are included in the back section of the book.

Why Tags? you might ask. We started seeing tags as art several years ago in the pages of Victoria magazine with the beautiful artwork of Sarah Lugg. It was probably her artwork that started the craze. Tags started to be seen on scrapbook pages, greeting cards and other paper crafts. Originally, artists were purchasing shipping tags and labels from their local stationery stores. Now every kind of tag imaginable is available to paper artists from craft, rubber stamp, paper and scrapbooking stores.

We hope that the ideas, designs and techniques on the following pages will inspire you to create your own tags to add to your various projects. You'll be amazed at how much fun it is to create with tags.

1

TABLE OF CONTENTS

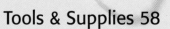

Designed by Nancy Ravenhall Johnson

This talented paper artist is employed as the graphic designer for a cultural museum. Working there influences the way Nancy looks at the world. She's also a basket maker and is drawn to the endless combination of techniques and materials that are found in nature.

Then she discovered tags…"for me, they are spontaneous, fun, where one thing leads to another," Nancy says. "The results are unexpected, there is that element of surprise in how the finished piece will look, and there are so many materials to use."

She wanted her tag to reflect her love of natural materials, vanishing cultures and the environment that supports them. "It is my wish we become more aware and think about all the materials we use."

Nancy received her BS in Urban Administration from the University of Cincinnati, College of Design, Art, Architecture and Planning. She is a member of the Misti Washington Basketry and Gourd Guild. She lives in Santa Ana, California with her husband Paul, three dogs and a parrot.

Supplies used:
Shipping tag
Assorted papers
Colored pencils
Silver brads
Image: photo copy
Metallic paper
Red willow sticks (from a friend's garden in Taos, New Mexico)
Feathers (from her pet Macaw, Gizmo)
Raffia
Stamp: Texture #63196 (Santa Rosa), Wishbone (StampaBarbara)
Gold ink stamp pad (Color Box)
Lettering, peg alphabet (Restoration Hardware)
Small glassine envelope

1. Affix the assorted papers to the tag using Sobo glue. (Refer to photograph for placement of papers.)

2. Tear three small metallic squares and glue to tag.

3. Stamp the papers with the textured stamp and gold ink.

4. Cut another piece of cardstock to make the pocket. Attach to the tag using brads.

5. Glue a larger metallic square and "hand" image to the pocket. Stamp with textured stamp and gold ink.

6. Add pencil accents around each layer of paper.

7. Poke small holes on one side of the pocket and thread with raffia. Glue on the feather.

8. Cut a narrow strip of striped gold and russet paper. Stamp the word "wish" using gold ink on half of the strip and glue to the tag.

9. Print an image of your choice on metallic paper. Cut out and stamp with the wishbone image in gold ink. Place this in the pocket.

10. Add willow sticks to the pocket.

11. Thread raffia through the hole in the tag and tie.

12. Stamp the wishbone image on the back of the tag. Glue the glassine envelope over the image.

(The wishbone was also stamped on the back of the tag with a small glassine envelope glued over the top. The wishbone appears to be inside the envelope.)

WISH

First Place

This tag was chosen as the first place prize winner because of the wonderful quality of the design. The innovative addition of the pocket which holds the haunting image was quite breathtaking. The back of the tag includes a glassine envelope displaying the symbolic wishbone design. Feathers, twigs and brads add dimension to this prizewinner.

Photo by
Chris Rainier

Designed by Kerri Judd

Kerri is a self taught muralist, illustrator and collage artist who lives in Huntington Beach, California. She should be an inspiration to others, because even though she has not had a lot of formal artistic training, she was able to sell her tag designs to a company that has had them printed. The tags are distributed to retail stores nationally and she'll have a new line of tags coming out in the spring of 2005. She was inspired to create her piece "Fashion Plate" because she needed a framed piece to hang on an empty wall in her new bedroom. She selected the background paper to go along with her color scheme. She found the frame at a yard sale for 50 cents!!

Supplies used:

3 shipping tags
Red decorative paper for background
Fabric
Cutout form (magazine piece)
Typewriter keys
Measuring tape embellishments
Chalk

Sparkling H20's, Old Gold
Red and black ink stamp pads
Lettering, Dream Quotes #636514
  (K & Company)
Stamps: dress form and shoe
  (Nature's Blessing), 123 Measurement,
  Romantic Swirl #B-18-107-C
  (Postmodern Design)
Black cardstock
Pinking shears
2 gold stars
Glue gun and glue sticks
Frame

1. Cover back of frame with the decorative paper.

2. Cut three pieces of black cardstock a bit larger than the tags. Cut each corner diagonally.

3. Tag #1: Stamp with the swirl design and red ink. Outline the swirls using gold Sparkles. Glue cut-out form to the tag. Glue tag to black cardstock.

Tag #2: Use chalk to lightly color the tag. Cut a fabric strip using pinking shears. Stamp the shoe design on the paper. Affix the lettering over the paper. Glue the fabric, paper, two gold stars, and measuring tape to the tag (refer to photo). Glue tag to cardstock.

Tag #3: Lightly rub chalk over the tag. Stamp measuring tape image to the left side of the tag. Stamp the dress form design in the center of the tag using red ink. Glue a bit of fabric and a measuring tape embellishment to tag (refer to photo). Glue tag to cardstock.

4. Glue cardstock tags to the background.

5. Glue on typewriter keys (refer to photo).

6. Frame the piece.

Our second place prize winner is this very whimsical and nostalgic framed piece. It illustrates nicely how tags can be incorporated into a truly handsome piece of wall art.

HARVEST HAIKU

Third Place

In third place is this very beautiful card displaying autumnal leaves, subtle use of colors and interesting papers in muted shades. Lovely ribbons cascade along the edge of the foliage-strewn card. A meaningful haiku is the greeting. The envelope accompanying this card is just as beautiful—an added bonus.

Supplies used:
Cardstock, light green
Mulberry paper, light green
Hang tag, 1½" x 3"
Shipping tag 4½" x 6"
Small jewelry tag
Fibers
Variegated ribbon, ¼" wide
Velveteen leaves
Stamps: Crane #2139F (JudiKin), Chinese
  Newspaper #1610, Bamboo Seal #H2080
  and Friendship Alphabet (Hero Arts)
Bronze ink stamp pad (Ink It)
Metallic ink stamp pad #UM-8 (Encore)
Deckle Edge scissors (Fiskars)
Maple leaf punch (Marvy Uchida)

1. Fold 8½" x 11" piece of cardstock and mulberry paper in half. Trim the right edge of the card using deckle edge scissors.

2. Using metallic ink, stamp randomly on the card the crane, chinese newspaper and bamboo images.

3. Place the mulberry paper on the inside of the card and tie on using the ribbons and fibers. Punch holes in the leaves and thread the ribbon on both inside and outside of the card.

4. Punch the maple leaf on the small jewelry tag and tie with fibers to the card.

5. Trim all around the large tag using the deckle edge scissors. Stamp this tag using the same three stamps as above and bronze ink.

6. Glue the fabric leaves to the tag (referring to photo).

7. Thread ribbon through the hole of the tag and glue the tag to the card.

8. Glue leaves to the inside of the lower right corner of the card.

9. Stamp the smaller tag with the Chinese newsprint using UM-8 pigment.

10. Use the alphabet stamp and bronze ink to stamp the first word of the haiku or quotation. Handwrite the rest.

11. Thread the ribbon through the tag and glue it above the leaf.

Designed by Elizabeth Zurkan

The beautiful seaside town of Dana Point, California is the home of paper artist, Elizabeth Zurkan. Since she was a little girl, she's always loved art and design. She considers herself self-taught, although she has taken classes in art appreciation as well as basic drawing. Her friends have been the lucky recipients of her handcrafted greeting cards that she's been creating for the past 10 years.

"The Harvest Haiku card was inspired by the changing seasons," she said. Fall is her favorite time of the year and her current interest is Japanese poetry.

Designed by Anita Byers

A love of art was instilled in Anita at an early age. "I won a prize for my painting in kindergarten and have been hooked on art ever since" she told us. But then her parents wanted her to study something practical like typing. Ironically these two talents have come together since she's now the customer service rep at Stampington Magazine and a featured designer for Stampington as well as Somerset Studio. She strongly believes that her interest in artistic exploration was responsible for her recovery from Stage 4 ovarian cancer.

Anita's European themed tags were inspired because of her love of Paris. She and her husband, Tom, make their home in Huntington Beach, California.

Supplies used:
Shipping tags
Stamps, Circus Diamonds #4404 and Parisian design Modes #DF4520 (Hampton Art Stamps)
Ink stamp pads: Yellow Cadmium, Azurite, Chestnut Roan, Blue Lagoon, Peach Pastel (Color Box)
Peach sheer ribbon, ¼" wide
Eiffel Tower (dimensional paper)

1. Antique the tags using various colors of ink directly to the tags.

2. Stamp the Parisian image and diamond design in colors of your choice.

3. Affix the Eiffel Tower to the tag using glue.

4. Tie the ribbon through the hole in the tag.

(The other two tags in this series represent England and Italy with appropriate charms and stamps.)

PARIS LONDON ROME

Luxury liners and exotic ports...grand hotels, palaces and monuments—
these are the subjects displayed on this original project. In lieu of a
travel journal, this collection of tags serves as a remembrance of a
European trip. The three tags display stamped images of each country
visited as well as dimensional embellishments to add interest. The
antiqued edges of the tags symbolize a bygone era of world travel.

LOVE IN PINK & BLUE

The small child staring out from the front of this card is a sweet image. As a birthday card, special greeting or just a note card, this charming card would certainly touch the recipient's heart. The metallic embossing powder and shiny silver charm combine to form this lovely design.

Supplies used:
Shipping tag, 2" x 4½"
Ivory cardstock, 5½" x 8"
Metallic blue ink stamp pad (Encore)
Stippling brush
Natural sea sponge
Malted Mauve Ink stamp pad (VersaMagic)
Stamp, Lines and Dots #1.0228 (Magenta)
Silver embossing powder (B'Muse)
Texture Tool
Diamond Glitter Glue (Sparkles)
Photocopy of young girl (could be a family portrait)
Silver ribbon
Love charm

1. For the tag: Sponge mauve ink onto the tag using a damp natural sea sponge. Let dry.

2. Stamp the lines and dot image to the tag. Emboss with silver embossing powder.

3. Use the texture tool dipped in blue to create tiny dots all over the tag.

4. Glue the "little girl" image on the tag. Highlight with glitter glue.

5. Tie the ribbon through the hole. Tie the silver ribbon through the charm and glue to the tag.

6. For the card: Cut the cardstock to 5½" x 8". Fold in half.

7. Use the stippling brush to apply the blue ink to the card front.

8. Glue the tag to the front of the card.

Designed by Patti Victoria Crump

Patti calls herself the "glitter queen". She thinks that a project isn't complete until the glitter is added. Originally from Canada, Patti now makes her home in West Hollywood, Calif. She became interested in crafts early on with the influence of her mom, art teachers and counselors from a local church.

"I am always on a quest to learn and I really enjoy sharing and studying different techniques and trading ideas with others," she said. This talented stamp artist believes that hidden inside all of us is a great artist and that art is a universal language.

Each of her tags were inspired by new techniques she has learned either from the internet, reading books and magazines, or watching cable television shows.

MY TAGS

Designed by Brian Dewar

Supplies used:
Manila file folder
Decorative paper, stripe
Peach and pink cardstock
6 small tags
Alphabet stamps
Black ink stamp pad
Large hole punch
String
Brass corners

1. Cut the manila folder large enough to hold your own tag collection. Glue the stripe paper to the front of the folder.

2. Fold the folder in half and then fold into a "V" (refer to photo on next page).

Punch three holes along the center of the fold.

3. Cut the pink/peach paper in a tag shape. Punch holes in each end. Stamp the small tags using alphabet stamps to spell "my tags" and glue to the peach tag. Glue the peach tag to the front of the folder. Thread the string through each hole and wrap to the inside front of the folder. Glue a strip of paper over the string to secure.

4. Add brass corners to each corner of the folder.

5. Thread your tag collection using string through the holes in the fold of the folder.

What a great way to store your collection of tags. As you learn new techniques, try different supplies, create memorable designs, you'll want to keep track of your progress. You might like to date each tag so that you can look back and gauge your progress as a tag artist.

It was so nice to receive a submission to this book from one lone man. Brian Dewar is a multi-media artist who resides with his wife Kaye in Yucaipa, California. He enjoys exploring innovative materials such as the encaustic wax technique which can be seen on some of the tags contained in his portfolio. A class by Bev Brazelton on this technique was the partial inspiration for this project. A fellow artist suggested the book format to contain his collection of tags. Brian is also a book artist and has created over 100 handcrafted books. Some of his work will be seen in upcoming issues of Somerset Studio Gallery 4 and the Somerset Red issue.

Designed by Mary Valleau

Mary would like to credit her many creative friends and local stamp shops for any talent seen in her work. "My friends have been tireless in offering excellent advice and inspiration," she said. She recommends joining stamping clubs as a way to keep diligent. She feels that being involved in a group helps one to stick with the projects and to push through them when the techniques are new and difficult. Mary works as an Engineering Technician for a county government office.

Supplies used:
Paper: ivory, black, brown, white cardstock
Decorative background paper
Gold metallic paper
Stamps: Animals (Magenta), Camel Collage #59-823 (StampaRosa, Tin Can Mail), Sphinx, Small Camel, Trail of Camels
Tag Punch (Emagination)
Pop Dots
Small hole punch (McGill hand punch)
Distress Ink, Vintage Photo and Antique Linen (Ranger)
Adirondack Ink, Butterscotch
Raffia
Small scallop edge scissors (Fiskars)

1. For the mini camel stamp: Use a square punch to create a 1¼" square of black cardstock. Trim with the scallop-edge scissors. Stamp the camel portion of the stamp on white cardstock. Punch out with 15/16" McGill square punch.

2. Color with markers and paint as follows: pyramid – Golden Wheat, sky – Eucalyptus, camel – Mocha, harness – gold gel pen, trees – green glaze pen.

3. Edge the image with gold gel pen and glue to the black square.

4. For the card: Stamp the giraffe image on white cardstock using Vintage Photo ink. Color with chalk: sky – blue, trees – forest green, pyramids – butterscotch. Touch up with markers.

5. For the small tag: Punch tag out of ivory cardstock using the Emagination punch. Punch a small hole in the top of the tag. Stamp using the sphinx-pyramid image and Vintage Photo ink.

6. Thread raffia through the hole.

7. Use a Pop Dot to attach the camel stamp to the larger image. Glue the tag just under the stamp.

8. Layer and glue the stamped image to the gold paper, decorative paper, brown, black then to the folded card.

9. Stamp the camel trail image along the right edge of the decorative paper using black ink.

ANIMALS OF EGYPT

A story is told here of an oasis teeming with animal life, white sands, tall palms and distant pyramids. Layers of decorative papers lend interest and the faux stamp and tiny tag create dimension. This card is almost too special to give away.

BON VOYAGE CARD

Designed by Patti Victoria Crump

Here's the perfect send-off for a friend casting off and setting sail for distant lands. The look of yesteryear is achieved with the addition of antiquing inks and vintage images.

Supplies used:
Shipping tag
Stamps: Compass #6585H (JudiKins), Regina 'd Italia
  #P01-103-F (Postmodern Designs), Column #61-801
  (Stampers Anonymous), Key (Sunday International),
  Italian Poetry Background #S1832 (Hero Arts)
Brown ink stamp pad, Art Print (Ranger)
Embossing powder, clear and gold
Cranberry and butterscotch ink (Adirondacks)
Black ink stamp pad (Versafine)
Natural sea sponge
Cardstock: black and ivory
Glue dots
Kraft colored raffia
Distress Ink, Walnut (Ranger)

1. For the Tag: Stamp on the white cardstock the compass design in brown ink, the Regina 'dItalia in cranberry, the column in Butterscotch. Emboss all with clear embossing powder.

2. Stamp the key design. Detail with gold embossing powder.

3. Cut out each image.

4. Stamp the tag with the Italian poetry background design using black ink.

5. Age the tag using the sea sponge and Butterscotch ink.

6. Cut out a tag from black cardstock slightly larger than the shipping tag.

7. Glue the tag to the black tag and adhere to the shipping tag using glue dots.

8. Tie the tag with kraft colored raffia.

9. For the card: Cut the ivory cardstock 8½" x 5½" and fold in half.

10. Age the card using the sea sponge lightly soaked in Walnut Ink and sprinkle a few Walnut Ink crystals on top while still wet. Let dry about 15 minutes and then heat set. Brush off excess crystals.

11. Attach the tag to the card using glue dots.

Supplies used:
Shipping tag
Stamps: Press Profile #C8408 (Stampington),
  Romantic Swirl #B18-107 (Post Modern Designs)
Persimmon Re-inker #33 (VersaMagic)
Purple ink stamp pad (Color Box)
Sepia archival ink
Diamond Glitter Glue
Foam dots (Stampa Rosa)
Gold embossing powder
Gold marker (Krylon)
Natural sea sponge
Heat gun
Beaded trim

1. For the tag: Cover the tag using the re-inker and a damp sea sponge. Let dry.

2. Stamp Pressed Profile floral design using purple ink.

3. While still wet, use your fingertips to pick up a small amount of gold embossing powder and sprinkle randomly over the flower image. Heat set.

4. Use the gold marker to edge the tag.

5. Glue beaded trim to the bottom edge of the tag.

6. For the card: Stamp the swirl design randomly to the ivory card using sepia ink.

7. When dry, highlight the swirls with glitter glue.

8. Attach the tag to the card using foam dots.

SWIRLS AND BEADS

Designed by Patti Victoria Crump

The random swirls decorate this card topped with the beautifully designed tag literally dripping with beads and fibers. This attractive card would surely brighten up the day of a friend who needs some cheering up.

TAG — YOU'RE IT

Designed by Pamela Renck

Pamela is a self-taught artist. She's always loved dabbling in painting, both acrylics and watercolors. She also enjoys creating trading cards and collage art. She was inspired to create "Tag – You're It" while watching her boys play tag. She put their love of the game together with her love of fairies and voila! the two ideas came together on her canvas. She wanted to try zetti-style art, a zany type of art that includes people and funky shapes. Pamela lives with her family in Anaheim, California.

What fun—a canvas literally exploding with color and liveliness. The charming paper dolls appear to be dancing through the tulips, their wings adding a touch of whimsy. This is another example of creating wall art from techniques used in paper arts.

Supplies used:

8" x 10" canvas
Golden acrylics: blue, green, yellow, red, white
Duo Adhesive
Jewels
Stamps: Sun (Anna Griffin for All Night Media), Dressmaker (Inkadinkado)
Mulberry paper
Copper ink stamp pad
Yellow Caran d'Ache crayon
Gold gel medium
3 shipping tags
Colored brads
Black ink stamp pad (Ancient Page)
Twinkling H20's
Butterfly and ladybug wings stickers (Color Box)
White cardstock
Faces (ArtChix)
Funky fibers
Small tag
Lavender Twinkling H20's
Alphabet stickers (Making Memories)
Pop Dots
Blue satin ribbon

1. Canvas: Paint the canvas with the acrylics: sky – blue, grass – green, flowers - dots of yellow and red, clouds - white.

2. Put Duo Adhesive where the jewels will be placed, then affix the jewels on the canvas.

3. Stamp the sun design on mulberry paper using Copper ink. Color the back with a yellow crayon. Place it on the canvas and seal it with Gold Gel Medium in soft Gel gloss.

4. For the fairy dolls: stamp the three large tags with the Dressmaker stamp in black ink.

5. Paint the tags with assorted Twinkling H20 colors. Once dry, cut them out.

6. Create the arms and legs using leftover tag pieces (refer to photo).

7. Press the butterfly and ladybug wings stickers onto a piece of white cardstock and cut them out.

8. Assemble the fairy bodies and attach the wings. Attach the arms and legs using colored brads.

9. Add the faces using the "face" collage sheets.

10. Wrap the fibers around the tag hole on the top of the fairy's heads.

11. Make the small tag by painting it lavender and adding the alphabet stickers. Attach the tag to the fairy with a piece of fiber.

12. Pose the fairies and attach them to the canvas using Pop-Dots.

13. Wrap blue ribbon around the edge of the canvas to give it a finished look.

DAVINCI TAG

This tag reminds us that there is art in all of us. Everyone has the ability to create. The da Vinci alphabet is displayed on torn squares of paper artistically applied along the side of the tag. Michelangelo's touching hands symbolically reach out across the tag. What a perfect piece to be displayed in an art studio as an inspiration for budding artists.

Supplies used:
Shipping tag, 3" x 6"
Stamps: Hands "Reaching Out" #M4159, Male
 Physique #R3146, Leaf and Letters #R3143
 (Stampington), Alphabet Set "da Vinci" #DF2205
 (Hampton Arts), "Create" #12015 (Art Impressions)
Inks: Brilliance Gold, Memories Soft Gold and
 Memories Artprint Brown
Assorted fibers in earthy colors

1. Stamp the Leaf and Letters background detail in various shades of gold.

2. Using darker shades of brown, stamp the "hands" as a focal point at the bottom.

3. Stamp "Create" on the left side of the tag.

4. Using all ink colors, sponge color all over the tag. Use a dark color to brush against the edges of the tag.

5. Stamp "A" "R" "T" on a piece of ivory paper. Tear around each letter. For texture and dimension, glue them randomly on the tag (see photo).

6. Thread the fibers through the hole of the tag and tie.

Designed by Nicole Steiman, the ARTbar

Nicole began playing with paper when she was a little girl. She's been stamping since 1992. She, along with her husband, Mark, opened the innovative ARTbar because of their shared passion for paper arts.

Together they have kept their focus constant— providing a hands-on place to create art.

Nicole and Mark live in Aliso Viejo, California with their 18 month old daughter, Josie.

Designed by Rachel Williams, the ARTbar

Being an art student at Mount San Antonio College in Walnut, California keeps Rachel busy. Not only does she take classes in drawing, painting, photography, print making and design, but she finds time in her busy schedule to manage the ARTbar. She's taken classes there as well. She particularly enjoyed workshops on doll making and paper making. Rachel resides in Chino Hills, California.

Supplies used:
Black/white upholstery fabric
Muslin fabric
Black button
Rubber stamp, alphabets
Rubber stamp, dress form (Nature's Blessing)
White thread
Black ink stamp pad (Stazon)
Black and white fiber

1. Cut two pieces of the black and white fabric to resemble a shipping tag. (Use a manila tag as a pattern and trace onto the fabric.) Sew the two pieces of fabric together loosely by hand.

2. Stamp the dress form and "dress up" on muslin fabric (refer to photo).

3. Cut, then layer the three pieces of muslin together (so that the upholstery fabric doesn't show through) and sew loosely onto the tag.

4. Sew a button to the top portion of the tag. Wrap the yarn around the button and tie to secure.

DRESS UP

Here's a switch—a tag made completely of fabric. Wouldn't this be the ideal hang-up for a sewing or craft room. The muslin attachment is stamped with a vintage dress form and fun alphabets displayed along the side. The fabric is sewn with a loose stitch to give a naïve appearance. This tag would also make a "fitting" gift for a seamstress friend.

GRAFFITI

Designed by Rachel Williams,
the ARTbar

Non-representational art is incorporated in this tag design. With the strong use of paint applied in an almost "Mark Rothko" technique, the tag is truly a work of modern art. Stamped in the corner is a mysterious "8". We can only guess the meaning of this number. This tag demonstrates techniques of graffiti art without having to practice on a wall!

Supplies used:
Shipping tag
Acrylic paint (Delta)
Foam alphabet and number stamps
  (Making Memories)
Magazine photo
Transfer ink (Superior)
Scrap piece of board
Blow pens (Color Workshop)
Black ink stamp pad (Stazon)

1. Use two to three colors of paint. Apply a small amount to the center of the tag. Use the scrap board to spread the paint around the tag creating a spare, blended painted surface.

2. Use Transfer Ink to distress the magazine picture by rubbing the ink on it until the image lifts up.

3. Glue this picture on the tag using a glue stick.

4. Repeat step 1 with a light neutral paint, covering some parts of the magazine picture.

5. Use the blow pen to blow ink around the tag creating a speckled surface.

6. Stamp a word or number as desired on the tag using black ink.

Supplies used:
¼" aluminum mesh (WireForm)
Binder clips, 1 large, 6 small
Keychains
5 tags (counter top sample chips)
Typewriter sticker #66026 (Memories in the Making)
Stamps: Harlequin (Rubber Stampede), Alphabets
  (Hero Arts)
Typewriter key stickers (EK Success)
Decorative papers, assorted (Memories in the Making)
Photocopies of vintage typewriters, etc.
Black ink stamp pad

1. Cut the screen to 10" x 11" using an old pair of scissors.

2. Stamp "So Long Typewriter" on the typewriter tag sticker using the alphabet stamps.

3. Cut around the image and clip it to the top of the screen using the large binder clip.

4. Decorate the sample chips using various torn pieces of paper, typewriter copies, harlequin stamp and typewriter key stickers.

5. Attach binder clips to each tag. Attach tags to screening either using bead chains or clips.

Here's a humorous farewell to an endangered species—the typewriter. The piece is designed with an industrial looking background. Each tag—actually countertop sample chips—have been embellished with bits of torn paper and images of vintage machines. Binder clips and keychains cleverly attach the tags to the screening. Typewriter key stickers add a further touch of nostalgia.

SO LONG TYPEWRITER

TAG BOOK

Displaying your tags

After you've experimented with several techniques you'll have a selection of beautiful tags to look back at and see your progress. You'll be able to refer to this collection again and again to give you inspiration. Each tag will make you think of something new to do for your next tag.

A simple way to make a "tag book" is to tie ribbons or fibers through the handy hole in the tag. You could also use a metal fastener to hold them together.

The tags in this "book" are samples of techniques taught at the ARTbar.

See page 14 for another example of displaying and cataloging your tags.

At the ARTbar you'll learn a myriad of tag making techniques. Once you've got a large collection to show off, you'll want to display them like this. Thread them together so you can easily view each and every one of your masterpieces.

YOU GOTTA HAVE HEART

Designed by
Rachel Williams,
the ARTbar

heart

Supplies used:
Shipping tag
Background paper or calligraphy
   stamp of your choice
Heart mold or stamp of your choice
Heart lettering, stamp of your choice
Homemade paper or air-dry clay
Red or burgundy pastels
Black ink stamp pad
Burgundy ribbon

1. Stamp a background on the tag or cover with a background paper.

2. Stamp homemade paper or air dry clay with a heart stamp or place in a mold.

3. Glue the paper or clay piece to the tag and color with pastels.

4. Stamp a small piece of paper with the lettering stamp. Affix to the tag.

5. Use a black ink pad to lightly brush the edges and bottom of the tag.

6. Thread ribbon through the hole of the tag and tie in a knot

Air dried clay is the special technique used to decorate this unique tag. The clay resembles handmade paper and is stamped or placed in a mold to achieve the dimensional heart design. The background can either be a stamp or decorative paper with a calligraphy design. The edges of the tag are antiqued with a slight brush of black ink.

Supplies used:
Shipping tag
Decorative paper with
  calligraphy design
Transfer Ink™
Image of girl
Ivory cardstock
Metallic foil sheets in Soft
  Pastels (Art Accentz)
Transfer Ink (Stewart
  Superior)
Heat N Stick powder
Stamp: Dare to Dream #M4672
  (Stampington)
Mauve ribbon, 2" wide

1. Cut the background paper to fit the tag and glue on using a glue stick.

2. Transfer the image using Transfer Ink by placing it face down onto ivory cardstock. Spray the back of the image and rub with a cottonball until the image transfers. It will be cloudy and blurred and look almost watercolored. Add additional coloring if desired.

3. After stamping only the "Dream" part of the stamp with pigment ink, sprinkle with Heat 'n Stick powder. Heat set with a heat gun. The powder will become a sticky adhesive. Place the foil (shiny side up) on top of the sticky letters. This is a fast and easy way to foil a stamped design.

4. To add foil accents around the layered picture, sponge pigment ink randomly around the edges of the image, then add Heat 'n Stick. Heat and then add the foil.

5. Glue the "dream" image to the tag and add ribbon.

DREAM

Designed by
Rachel Williams,
the ARTbar

CORINTHIANS

Designed by Nicole Steiman,
The ARTbar

Supplies used:
Shipping tag
Transparent laminate sheet (JudiKins)
Sea Spray Leaf (Amy's Magic)
Four brads
Distress inks: Walnut Stain and
  Old Paper (Ranger)
Stamp, Chinese calligraphy
  K-3394 (PSX)
Black ink stamp pad
  (Stazon)
Paintbrush
⅛" hole punch
Plastic container
  for foil

1. Distress the tag by rubbing the ink pad directly to the edges using the Walnut Stain and Old Paper inks.

2. Cut one piece of the laminating sheet about ½" smaller than the tag on the left, right and bottom sides and ½" from the hole on the top of the tag.

3. Take the backing off the laminate sheet and dip it in the gold leaf to completely cover it. Use the paintbrush to brush off the excess. Add more leaf if necessary to cover.

4. Turn it over and stamp the calligraphy image using black ink. Let the stamp impression dry for a few seconds.

5. Punch holes using the hand punch on all four corners of the sheet and tag.

6. Place small brads through the holes.

7. Add fibers and ribbon for final touches.

GEISHA

The far east is the subject of this exotic tag. The lovely geisha image is displayed along with an Asian coin. Both small and large Asian calligraphy stamps were used to decorate the tag. The transparent laminate collects the layer of variegated leaf to add a burnished warmth to this fascinating design.

Supplies used:
Shipping tag, 3" x 6"
Stamps, small and large Asian characters
Black ink stamp pad
Distress Ink, Walnut (Ranger)
Brown cardstock
4 small brads
Transparent laminate sheet (JudiKins)
Variegated gold leaf
Asian coin charm (Memories in the Making)
Gold ribbon, ¼" wide
Small paintbrush
Spray fixative
Small hole punch
Glue gun and glue stick
Geisha print

1. Stamp the small Asian characters using the walnut ink to completely cover the tag.

2. Glue on the brown card stock (cut smaller than the tag), then the geisha print.

3. Take the backing off the laminate sheet and dip it in the gold leaf to completely cover it. Use the paintbrush to brush off the excess. Add more leaf if necessary to cover.

4. Turn it over and stamp the larger Asian characters using black ink. Spray with fixative and allow to dry.

5. Punch all four corners and attach it to the tag with the small brads.

6. Glue on the Asian coin with the glue gun.

7. Tie on the ribbon

SO LITTLE TIME

Designed by Anita Byers

Supplies used:
Shipping tag
Black ink stamp pad (Stazon)
Stamp: clocks #G-3570 (PSX)
Glitter Glue, orange and green (Sparkles)
Stamp pads in assorted colors (ColorBox)
Cosmetic sponge
Multi-colored fibers

So many tags…so little time!! This tag reminds us that we'd like to have an unlimited amount of time in which to create as many masterpieces as possible. A collection of various timepieces, watch parts and clock faces are stamped in a variety of interesting shades to create this timeless piece.

1. Use a cosmetic sponge to apply the assorted ink colors to the tag to create a soft light application of color.

2. Stamp the clock images using various colors of ink.

3. Trace over the details of the images using contrasting glitter colors.

4. Tie the fibers through the hole of the tag.

ECO ART IN A BOX

Supplies used:
Page tags (Eco Africa)
Various embellishments (Eco Africa)
Corrugated paper
Stamps: Petroglyph designs
Brown ink stamp pad
Pigment brush stamp pads, various
   colors (Color Box)
Lumiere paints, Super Copper and
   Pearl Blue (Jacquard)
Paintbrush
4 cup hooks
Wooden crate
Hole punch

1. The tags from Eco Africa are available with layers of handmade papers already attached. Embellish them with various seeds, beads, paper flowers, and other naturals.

2. Stamp the petroglyph designs in brown randomly to the tags.

3. Cut four pieces of corrugated paper a bit larger than the tags. Use the pigment brush pads in colors of your choice to "paint" the top edges of the corrugated strips.

4. Glue the decorated tags to the corrugated strips. Punch a hole in the top of the strips.

5. Paint around the edge of the crate using the Lumiere paints.

6. Attach cup hooks through the top of the crate and hang the tags on each hook.

MY DEAR GIRL

A scrap of an old letter was the inspiration for this nostalgic design. Who was writing to "My Dear Girl"—an old beau, a caring parent, or a new love? We can only guess who the correspondent was. It certainly lends an air of mystery to this intriguing tag displaying scrollwork background, bits of vellum and a beautiful portrait of the dear girl.

Supplies used:
Vellum square tag, 2" x 2"
Shipping tag, 3" x 6"
Green sheer ribbon, 1½" wide
Stamp, Ornamental (All Night Media)
Dark green ink stamp pad
Green vellum (Memories in the Making)
Postage stamp stickers (Memories in the Making)
Photocopy of old-fashioned girl
Photocopy of calligraphy (old letter)
Glue stick

1. Use the scroll stamp and dark green ink to cover the background of both tags.

2. Glue the copy of the old-fashioned girl to the center of the vellum tag using a glue stick.

3. Press stamp sticker over the picture.

4. Tear the letter piece and green vellum into small pieces to fit on the tag. Glue on using a glue stick.

5. Press the stamp sticker over the green vellum piece.

6. Thread ribbon through the hole of the tag and knot.

LAVENDER FIELDS

You can almost smell the aroma of the lavender fields in Provence. A tiny bit of the aromatic blossom is the focal point of this ephemeral tag. Lovely calligraphy serves as a background, while sheer ribbon encases the bit of lavender. A touch of thread winds gracefully around the tag as a fitting embellishment.

Supplies used:

Shipping tag, 2½" x 6"
Stamps: Text Thin (A Stamp in the Hand), Hydrangea by Anna Griffin (All Night Media)
Dried lavender
Ink stamp pads: green, lavender and black
Twinkling H20's: green and lavender
Small paintbrush
Purple wired thread (May Arts)
Sheer lavender ribbon, 2" wide
Craft glue and glue gun

1. Stamp the tag with the text design using black ink.

2. Stamp the hydrangea using lavender ink and the leaves using green.

3. Using a paintbrush, highlight the flower petals and the leaves with the Twinkling H20's.

4. Glue the dried lavender on the bottom portion of the tag using craft glue.

5. Wrap the 2" sheer ribbon around the bottom of the tag and glue to the back to secure.

6. Wrap the purple thread around the tag twice and hot glue to the back.

7. Thread the ribbon through the hole of tag and tie.

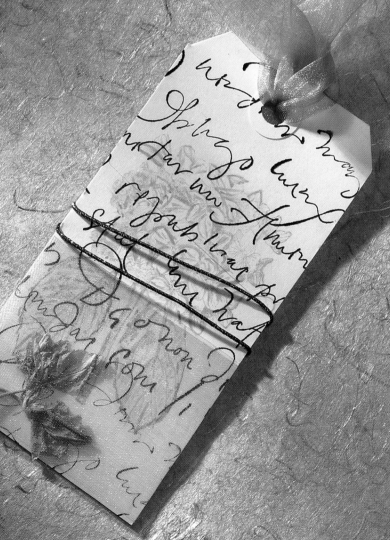

41

TRIPTYCH

Supplies used:

3 shipping tags, 3" x 6"
Stamp, Foliate cube (Stampendous)
Ink stamp pads: forest green, rust, purple metallic
3 photocopies of vintage photos
Gold wire ribbon

Small scrap of screen
3 small brads
Rusty star
Small hole punch
Square hole punch
Dark brown paper strips, Decorative Accents (Black Ink)
Glue stick
Glue gun

1. Stamp the three tags with three types of foliage from the cube stamp using the three ink colors.

2. Glue one photo to each tag.

3. Punch several square holes on the left side of one of the tags. Weave the gold ribbon through the holes.

4. Fasten the scrap of screen to one of the tags using the brads.

5. Glue on the rusty star using the glue gun.

6. Lay the three cards flat and tape them together using the paper strips and glue stick.

PROMISE

Supplies used:
Tag, 3" x 6"
Stamps: Ornamental (All
   Night Media), Honor Bound
   #G2-AA677 (Acey Deucy)
Ink stamp pad, Metallic Purple
   (Encore), Forest Green
Feather
Scrap of linen fabric
Green Ivy vellum (Memories
   in the Making)
Blue embroidery floss and
   needle
Small hole punch
Satin ribbon, 2" wide
Pinking shears
Feather charm (Memories in
   the Making)

1. Stamp all around the outside edge of the tag with the Ornamental stamp and metallic ink.

2. Cut the green vellum with the pinking shears to fit the middle of the tag and glue it on.

3. Stamp the eye design on a small piece of linen using forest green ink. Cut it out using pinking shears. Glue it at the bottom of the vellum. Tuck the feather under it before gluing down.

4. Punch tiny holes on the left side of the vellum and linen piece. Sew the blue floss through the holes.

5. Use a glue gun to glue on the feather charm.

6. Thread the ribbon through the hole of the tag.

WOMAN WITH BASKET

Supplies used:
Shipping tag, 3" x 6"
Black/white check ribbon
Stamp: Harlequin (Rubber Stampede)
Black ink stamp pad
Gold Sparkles (PSX)
Butterfly & feather stickers (Memories in the Making)
Green vellum (Memories in the Making)
Green print paper napkin
Glue stick
Photocopy of girl
Black photo corners

1. Stamp the harlequin design on the tag using black ink.

2. Cut a strip of the green napkin ½" wide and glue to the left edge of the tag.

3. Cut the photocopy to fit in the center of the tag. Affix black photo corners to the top of the photocopy. Glue to the tag.

4. Spread the gold sparkles over the stamped design.

5. Stamp the harlequin design on the bottom portion of the vellum paper.

6. Tear the vellum paper to fit the tag. Glue it over the bottom of the photocopy of the girl.

7. Attach the stickers (see photo)

8. Glue a piece of the ribbon along the bottom edge of the tag. Tie another piece of ribbon through the hole of the tag.

DRAGONFLY

Supplies used:
Shipping tag, 2½" x 5"
Burgundy paper strips,
   Decorative Accents (Black Ink)
Stamp: Swan Woman #1814
   (Just for Fun)
Black ink stamp pad
Metallic acrylics: Silver, Russet
   (Lumiere)
Corrugated cardboard
Twinkling H20's, Olive Vine
   (LuminArte)
Green nubby yarn

1. Pour out a little puddle of metallic silver and rust on a piece of glass. Let them run together a little. Place the tag face down on the paint (try this first on scrap paper). Move it around to apply paint in several places. Allow to dry.

2. Stamp the dragonfly section of the stamp on the tag.

3. Glue the burgundy paper strips around the outside edge of the tag. Stamp more dragonflies all around the edge of the tag.

4. Use a fine spray to wet the Sparkling H20's and let sit until it's a thickish consistency to load on a brush. Brush a thick pool of this onto the piece of glass or paper plate. Press a scrap of corrugated cardboard into the paint and use it as a stamp to stamp all over the tag and onto the borders.

5. Thread the yarn through the hole of the tag and tie.

FRIDA

Supplies used:
Shipping tag, 3" x 6"
Stamps: coil design (Rubber Poet),
Frida #1902 (A Stamp in the Hand)
Silver cross charm from Mexico
Black ink stamp pad
Pigment brush stamp pads: green,
  blue, red, yellow and lavender
  (Color Box)
Wired thread: various colors
  (May Arts)
Twinkling H20's, matching ink pad
  colors
Small paintbrush
Glue gun and glue sticks

1. Rub the ink pads (excluding black) across the tag for a rainbow effect.

2. Stamp the coil design to the tag using assorted ink colors.

3. With a small brush and matching colors of Twinkling H20's, outline the coils.

4. Stamp the Frida design in the center of the tag using black ink.

5. Glue the cross to the tag using the glue gun.

6. Cut the wired thread into different lengths. Thread them through the hole of the tag and tie. Curl the wire by wrapping it around a pencil.

Colorful swirls decorate the background of this tag dedicated to artist, Frida Kahlo. The silver cross from Mexico adds dimension to this ethnic charmer. Wild and wonderful wired thread curls this way and that to top a tag loaded with inspiration.

BEADS AND FLOWERS

Supplies used:
Shipping Tag, 3" x 6"
Vellum tag, 1½" x 2½"
Purple marble paper, #61224
  (Memories in the Making)
Small glass beads, assorted colors
Stamp, Ornamental #2403R
  (All Night Media) –
Ink stamp pads, clear pigment
Embossing powder: turquoise,
  lavender and rust
Heat gun
Fuzzy yarn
Glue
stick
Craft
glue

1. Cut marble paper the same size as the tag and glue to the tag.

2. Stamp the design along one side of the tag using clear pigment ink.

3. Pour the different colors of embossing powder over the ink (do this one design at a time). Emboss using the heat gun.

4. Stamp the vellum tag in the same way and emboss.

5. Glue the beads along one side of the vellum tag.

6. Thread the yarn and the string of the vellum tag through the hole of the tag and tie.

YOU'RE INVITED TO TEA

Supplies used:
Shipping tag, 3" x 6"
Stamp: You're Invited #51316 (Hero Arts)
Photocopies: tea pot, tea picture
Charms: tea pot, tea bag, spoon and cups
  (Memories in the Making)
Wired thread, various colors (May Arts)
Rose stickers (Memories in the Making)
Paper doily
3 gold jump rings
Needlenose pliers
Black ink stamp pad
Deckle edge scissors
Gold cord
Hole punch
Hot glue gun and glue stick

1. Stamp the "You're Invited" design to the tag.

2. Cut the tea party image using deckle edge scissors. Cut out the tea pot image. Glue both to the tag.

3. Cut a small piece of the paper doily and glue to the tag. Glue a tea cup and a spoon charm over the doily.

4. Glue the charms to the tag using the glue gun (refer to photograph).

5. Press the rose stickers to the tag (see photo)

6. Punch three holes evenly spaced at the bottom of the tag. Thread the jump rings and tea cup charms through the holes. Close the jump rings using needlenose pliers.

7. Thread the gold cord through the hole in the tag and tie.

THINKING OF YOU

Supplies used:
Shipping tag, 3" x 6"
Stamp: Thinking of You
  (Westwater Enterprises)
Charms: thimble and
  scissors (Memories in
  the Making)
Button card and sewing
  trade card photocopies
Ink stamp pads:
  turquoise and gold
Deckle edge scissors
Green yarn

1. Lightly rub the turquoise stamp pad over the tag.

2. Rub the edges of the tag using the gold ink pad.

3. Cut around the sewing trade card with deckle edge scissors, ¼" in from the tag edge.

4. Glue the image, as well as the button card image to the tag.

5. Stamp "Thinking of You" in the corner.

6. Glue on the charms (refer to photo).

7. Thread the yarn through the hole of the tag and tie.

Your mother or aunt would appreciate this greeting. Decked out with a combination of sewing tools, this tag displays a thimble, scissors, and a card of buttons. Added to that is a charming copy of an old fashioned trade card advertising thread. Any seamstress would love to receive a themed card such as this.

BEADED LADIES

Supplies used:
Shipping tag, 3" x 6"
Pigment brush pads: Terra Cotta, Orchid, Lavender
Glitter beads
Clear double-sided Tape (Terrifically Tacky)
Vintage print of two ladies
Stamp: Bow by Anna Griffin (All Night Media)
Oval template
Glitter Glue: Diamond and Gold (Sparkles by PSX)
Black ink stamp pad
Twinkling H20: Blue
Pearl-edged ribbon, 1" wide

1. Brush the three colors of pigment all over the tag and blend together.

2. Place the oval template on the print and trace around with a pencil.

3. Put clear double-sided tape over the area you've penciled in and then cut around the line.

4. Tape or glue the print to the tag. Pour the glitter beads onto the tape. Pour off the excess and retain.

5. Stamp the bow design with black ink under the oval. Paint it blue using the Twinkling H20's. Dot all around it with the diamond Glitter Glue.

6. Outline around the oval with gold Glitter Glue.

7. Tie on the ribbon.

A shimmering composite of transparent beads lends luster to these Victorian beauties. A pearlescent blue bow dotted with glitter embellishes this lustrous cameo. Threading its pretty way through the top of the tag is a frothy sheer ribbon.

SUPER PEARL

Supplies used:
Shipping label, 3" x 6"
Photocopy of button card
Stamp: Ornamental (All Night Media)
Black/gold paper (Anna Griffin)
Black ink stamp pad
Gold paper
5 tiny white buttons
Needle and white thread
White embroidery floss
Deckle edge scissors

A photocopy of a button card is the central theme of this unique tag. Layered on gold decorative paper and surrounded with scrollwork designs, the buttons pictured are mimicked by real ones randomly scattered on the tag.

1. Cut a piece of gold paper ⅛" larger than the button card photocopy, and with the deckle edge scissors, cut a piece of black and gold patterned paper ¼" larger than the gold.

2. Layer and glue the photo copy on the gold paper and then on the black/gold paper.

3. Glue this layered piece on the tag.

4. Stamp the top and bottom of the tag with the scroll design.

5. Randomly sew buttons to the tag using the needle and thread.

6. Separate the 6 strands of floss into 4 strands and wrap around the tag. Glue the ends of the floss on the back to secure.

JOURNEY

Supplies used:
Shipping tag, 3" x 6"
Stamp: Dragonfly #246 (Hampton Art)
Black ink stamp pad
Gold ribbon
Bronze glitter glue: Sparkles by PSX

Distress Ink: Vintage Photo (Ranger)
Black card stock
Brass button
"journey" ribbon (7 Gypsies)
Gold paper
Gold ribbon
Square hole punch
4 brass brads
Variegated gold leaf
Brush
Transparent laminating sheet (JudiKins)

1. Rub the Distress Ink all over the tag.

2. Stamp the dragonfly design randomly to the tag using black ink.

3. Fill in the wings of the dragonflies using bronze glitter glue.

4. Pour a bit of the multi-colored leaf on the adhesive side of the laminate sheet. With a paintbrush, brush it until only a thin layer remains. Punch holes in each corner and attach to the tag using bronze brads. Stamp the dragonfly design on the front of the sheet.

5. Cut two pieces of black card stock, 4" x 6", and 1½" x 4". Make a pocket by placing the short piece over the long. Punch around the outside edge of the short piece. Thread the bronze ribbon through the holes. Glue ends of the ribbon on the back to secure.

6. Apply the glitter glue over the black cardstock and rub with fingers to spread it.

7. Glue on two torn pieces of gold paper, the "journey" ribbon and brass button. Slip the tag into the pocket.

BEETHOVEN'S TENTH

Supplies used:
Shipping tag, 3" x 6"
Stamp: Composer cube (Post Modern Design) Music Score #14TJ (All Night Media)
Black ink stamp pad
White mulberry paper
Gold ribbon, ¼" wide
Gold net stretch ribbon
Paper Plus Decoupage Finish (Delta)

1. Gently rub the black ink pad over the tag to antique it. Do not cover the tag completely.

2. Stamp the music and composer on two separate pieces of mulberry paper. Tear around each image.

3. Layer the music and composer piece to the tag using decoupage medium.

4. When dry, stretch the gold net ribbon over the tag and glue onto the back.

5. Thread the gold ribbon through the hole in the tag and tie.

A brooding Beethoven stares from behind a gold chained ribbon on this tag dedicated to the great composer. A sheet of music forms the background of the tag that has been aged to perfection with the addition of black ink around the edges. You can almost hear strains of music coming from this original design.

GIFT TAG TRIO

Supplies used:
3 tags, 1½" x 3"
Assorted red/white papers
   (Memories in the Making)
Alphabet stickers (Memories
   in the Making)
Stamp: swirl design
Pigment brush pad: Terra Cotta
   (Color Box)
Ribbon, various designs

1. Rub the edges of the tags with the terra-cotta stamp pad.

2. Stamp the swirl design randomly on the tags also with the terra-cotta stamp pad.

3. Cut out the papers in the shape of the tag, just slightly smaller.

4. Glue the paper tags to the base tags.

5. Affix the alphabet stickers to each tag spelling out "just" "for" and "you".

6. Thread ribbons through the holes of the tags and tie all three onto a gift package.

Wouldn't a gift all wrapped up in red and white paper look fantastic with this trio of tags tied onto the top? Each of the three tags is a small gem, decorated with coordinating paper and a swirl stamp. The cheerful ribbons tying the tags complete this pretty picture.

VIVA LAS VEGAS

Supplies used:
Cardstock: pink, lavender, blue
3 hang tags: chartreuse (Waste Not Paper)
Small hole punch
Stamp: Funky Square #2 (JudiKins)
White paper
Font: Fun House
Black ink stamp pad
Deckle edge scissors
Paper strips: Decorative Accents (Black Ink)
Needle and black thread

1. Cut three pieces of the cardstock 5½" x 6". Cut three more pieces for the pockets the same size, cutting one edge on an angle (see photo).

2. Using the Funky stamp designs and black ink, stamp randomly on all the pieces of cut cardstock, alternating the designs.

3. Stamp the same designs on the tags.

4. Use a small hole punch to create holes around the edges of the pockets and backing cardstock. Sew each pair of pockets individually using needle and black thread.

5. Create CD labels for tags using computer font of choice or alphabet stamps on white paper. Cut one edge of labels using deckle edge scissors.

6. Glue the labels to each tag. Glue the tags to the pockets.

7. Use the paper tape to bind the three pockets together on the back using a glue stick.

8. Insert CD's of your choice.

SWAN WOMAN

Supplies used:
Linen fabric
Moon charm
Stamp: Ornamental (All Night Media),
   Swan Woman #E1814 (Just for Fun)
Needle and metallic floss (Kreinik)
Distress Ink, Walnut (Ranger)
White hole reinforcement
Pinking shears
Twinkling H20's: Sage, Cherry Sorbet,
   Summer Breeze, Icy Iris
Sheer lavender ribbon, 1" wide

1. Cut three layers of linen into a tag shape using pinking shears. (Use a shipping tag as a pattern and trace onto the fabric.)

2. Punch a hole at the top of the tag through both layers of fabric. Glue on a hole reinforcement using craft glue.

3. Stamp the woman design on the tag using the walnut ink.

4. Stamp the ornamental design on the bottom left side of the tag and the top right side along the edge using the walnut ink.

5. Paint around the outside edges of the design using the various shades of the Sparkling H20's.

6. Attach the ribbon to the tag and tie.

7. Thread metallic thread through the charm and tie to the hole of the tag.

MOTHER & CHILD

Supplies used:
Shipping tag, 3" x 6"
Encaustic wax: black, silver and red
Calligraphy stamp of your choice
Vintage images
Black ink stamp pad
Heat gun
Wire edged ribbon
Walnut ink (Ranger)

1. Crumble the tag in your hand.

2. Rub the walnut ink over it to give an aged appearance.

3. Smooth it out and stamp a calligraphy image with black ink to cover the whole tag.

4. Glue on a couple of vintage images.

5. Hold a heat gun near the encaustic wax and allow it to melt and drip on the tag in several places with various colors. Hold the tag up and move it around so that the wax runs together and spreads on the tag.

6. Thread a wire-edge ribbon through the hole in the tag and tie.

Tools

Rubber stamps

Tags come in many shapes, sizes and colors

Stamp pads, dye and pigment

Price tag

Printed tag on a sticker

Embossing powder

Some of the many glazes and varnishes

Vellum tags

Sparkling H20's water colors

Countertop sample chips can be used as tags

Glitter glue

Tie up your tag art with twine, yarn, ribbon and other fibers

Charms make great embellishments

Metallic paints

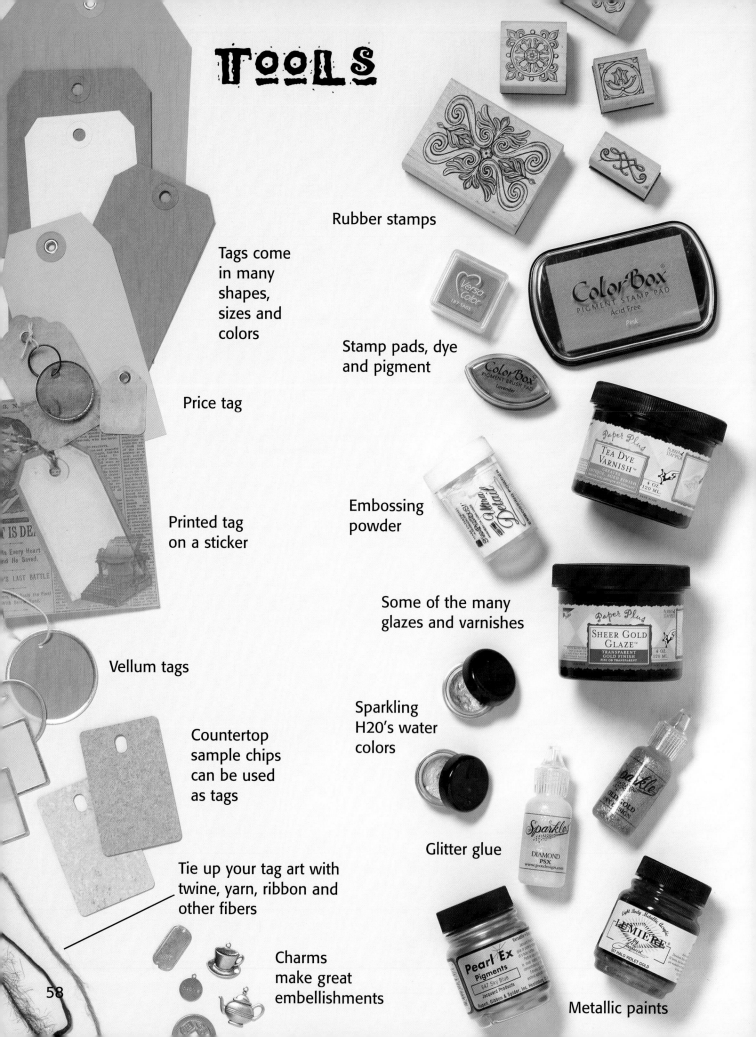

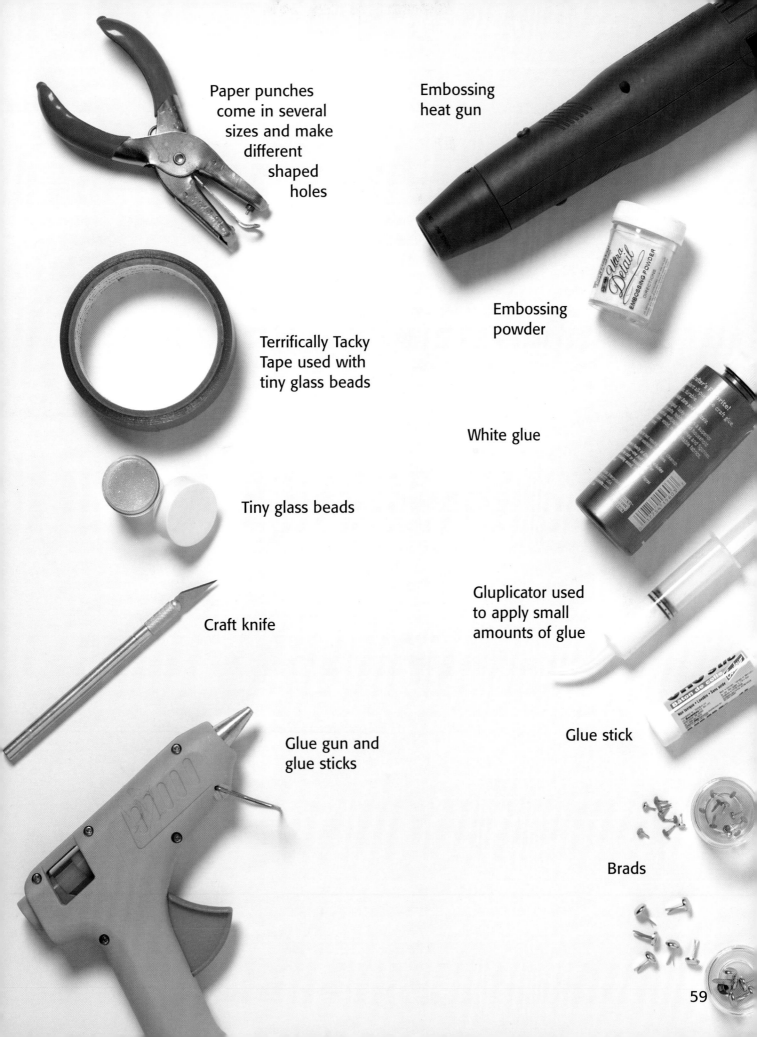

Paper punches come in several sizes and make different shaped holes

Embossing heat gun

Embossing powder

Terrifically Tacky Tape used with tiny glass beads

White glue

Tiny glass beads

Craft knife

Gluplicator used to apply small amounts of glue

Glue stick

Glue gun and glue sticks

Brads

TOOLS & TECHNIQUES

Dye ink pads

These are available in pre-inked pads (the traditional stamp pads that you're probably familiar with). They come in a large variety of colors, are water-based and quick drying. These inks are used for stamping on all papers.

Pigment ink pads

These also come in a wide variety of vivid colors. The ink is slow drying so these inks are typically used with embossing powders. The sponges on these pads sit above the base of the container so that they can be used to ink directly to any size stamp (rather than applying the stamp to the pad).

Pigment brush stamps (from Colorbox) are small oval stamp pads which can be used to decorate directly to the paper or directly to a stamp. They're easy to handle, come in lots of colors and are relatively inexpensive.

Dimensional glue

Diamond glaze is a water-based dimensional adhesive that is used directly over artwork for a raised, glass-like finish. When thinned with water it has a lacquer-like finish. Dye ink can be added to it to achieve custom colors. It's also used for gluing glitter, beads, glass, plastic and vellum to paper.

Decorating chalks

Chalks are used to shade and blend colors for a soft pastel finish. Applied with sponge applicators, the chalks can be layered or worked together to achieve a third color. They're acid free and non-toxic.

Dry brush markers

Markers can be used to color your stamped project on paper or you can color your rubber stamp directly with the marker (rather than using a stamp pad). Markers are especially useful when you want a multicolored look. You can use several different colors to paint directly on your stamp and then stamp to paper.

Re-inkers

Small bottles of dye or embossing inks that can be used to revitalize ink pads. They can also be used for watercoloring (just add a little water to the ink) or for painting directly on a stamp and then stamping onto paper. This gives you a loose, arty look.

Sparkling H20's

These pigment colors come in small containers and can be used to paint on paper or directly onto the stamp. Just apply a little spritz of water from a spray bottle before using. Creates a nice watercolor effect.

Metallic markers

Metallic markers are available in gold, silver, and bronze, etc. The gold leafing pen is useful for adding borders to cards, writing personal messages or for decorating polymer clay or air dry clay pieces.

Encaustic wax

For this technique, hold a heat gun near the wax and allow it to melt and drip in several places with various colors. Hold the tag up and move it around so that the wax runs together and spreads on the tag.

Inking a stamp

Apply the stamp on the dye-based pad. Then stamp it on a test piece of paper. Check to make sure that it stamped completely and that you didn't get any edges from the untrimmed part of the stamp. Keep trying until you get a nice clean image. Re-ink your stamp again and stamp on your project.

Another way to ink your stamp is with a colored marker. Color the complete image area or only part of the image. Or use different color markers on the stamp for a multi-colored look.

When using extra large stamps (such as background stamps) on a small project, you can ink your stamp and place your project directly onto the stamp to ink it.

Direct to paper inking technique

Use a stamp pad with a raised pad to decorate the paper. Gently rub the pad onto the paper or use a sponge. You can use more than one color to create different looks.

Staining and aging

There are several ways to achieve an aged look to your paper:

Direct to paper: Rub on dye ink with the pad or your finger (golds and browns work well).

Coffee: Brush on coffee using a paintbrush. Either brush it all over the paper or brush it in streaks. The same look can be achieved using Walnut Ink Crystals by PostModern Designs, the Distress Inks from Ranger, or Paper Plus Tea Dye Varnish from Delta.

Torn edges: a nice aged look is achieved when paper is torn around the edges. The torn edges can be left alone or colored with a pen or ink pad.

Embossing

To achieve a dimensional look to your project, first apply embossing ink to your stamp. Embossing ink is usually clear or slightly tinted. The embossing ink can either be on a pad or in a roller tube that you just roll onto your stamp. Then impress the image onto the surface.

Pour or shake embossing powder over the ink. Shake off the excess.

Heat the surface using a heat gun until the powder melts and becomes raised.

You can also use a dye ink pad for embossing, but this ink dries a lot faster, so you have to work much more quickly.

Try experimenting with embossing. You can use different colors of powders and metallics. You can mix colors of powders together for different effects. Embossing powders are available in different grades from detail, fine to double thick.

Air dry clay

This clay can be decorated the same as polymer clay, but it doesn't have to be baked. It's lighter weight so is useful in card marking. The clay can be decorated with markers or colored pencils, as well as with paints.

Additional supplies:

Hole punches
Decorative punches
Craft knife
Glitter glue
Metal ruler
Scissors
Decorative scissors
Scotch tape
Tweezers

SOURCES

All of the supplies used in this book are widely available in craft, rubber stamping, scrapbook, paper, and art materials shops. If you have problems finding these items, the following suppliers will be able to help you.

Rubber Stamps

A Stamp in the Hand
(310) 884-9700
www.astampinthehand.com

Acey Deucy
(518) 398-5108
www.LKPerrella.com

Anna Griffin stamps by
All Night Media
Plaid Enterprises
(678) 291-8100
www.plaidonline.com

Art Impressions
(800) 393-2014
www.artimpressions.com

Bunch of Fun
www.bunchoffun.com

Hampton Art Stamps
(631) 924-1335
www.hamptonart.com

Hero Arts
(510) 652-6055
www.heroarts.com

Inkadinkado
(781) 938-6100
www.inkadinkado.com

JudiKins
(310) 515-1115
www.judikins.com

Just for Fun
(727) 938-9898
www.jffstamps.com

Magenta
(405) 922-5253
www.magentarubberstamps.com

Making Memories
(801) 294-0430
www.makingmemories.com

Nature's Blessing
(734) 542-6016
www.naturesblessing.com

PSX
(707) 588-8058
www.psxdesign.com

Post Modern Designs
(405) 321-3176
postmoderndesign@aol.com

Rubber Poet
(800) 906-7638
www.rubberpoet.com

Rubber Stampede
(800) 423-4135
www.rubberstampede.com

StampaBarbara
www.stampabarbara.com

Stamp Francisco
Stampa Rosa
www.stampfrancisco.com

Stampendous
(800) 869-0474
www.stampendous.com

Stampers Anonymous
(440) 250-9112
www.stampersanonymous.com

Stampington & Company
(877) STAMPER
www.stampington.com

Sunday International
www.sundayint.com

Westwater Enterprises
(201) 935-6220
Email csabosik@westwat.com

Stamp Pads

Clearsnap
(360) 293-6634
(Pigment Brush pads by Color Box)

Ranger Crafts
www.rangerink.com
(Distress inks)

Paint

Delta Technical Coatings
(800) 423-4135
www.deltacrafts.com
(Paper Plus Tea Dye Vanish)

Krylon
(216) 566-2000
www.krylon.com

Jacquard Products
(707) 433-9577
www.jacquardproducts.com
(Lumiere paints)

LuminArte
(866) 229-1544
www.luminarteinc.com
(Sparkling H20s)

PSX
(707) 588-8058
www.psxdesign.com
(Sparkles Glitter Glue)

Caran d'Ache
www.carandache.ch

Tools

Color Workshop
(blow pens)

Fiskars
(715) 842-2091
www.fiskars.com
(Decorative edge scissors,
Paper punches)

Marvy/Uchida
(310) 793-2200
www.uchida.com
(paper punches)

Embellishments

Amaco/Wire Form
(800) 374-1600
www.amaco.com

Art Accents
(360) 733-8989
www.artaccents.net
(foil sheets)

Eco Africa
(888) 721-6323
www.ecoafrica-usa.net

Graphic Products Corp.
Black Ink
www.gpcpapers.com
(Decorative Accents paper strips)

K & Company
(816) 389-4150
www.kandcompany.com
(alphabet sheets)

Kreinik Mfg. Co. Inc.
(410) 281-0040
www.kreinik.com
(metallic floss)

May Arts
(203) 637-8366
www.mayarts.com
(ribbon)

Memories in the Making
Leisure Arts
(501) 868-8800
www.leisurearts.com
(charms)

7Gypsies
(480) 325-3358
www.7gypsies.com
(printed twill ribbon)

Paper & Stickers

Anna Griffin, Inc.
(404) 817-8170
www.annagriffin.com

EK Success
(800) 524-1349
www.eksuccess.com

Memories in the Making
Leisure Arts
(501)868-8800
www.leisurearts.com

Making Memories
(801) 294-0430
www.makingmemories.com

Adhesives

Delta Technical Coatings
(800) 423-4135
www.deltacrafts.com
(Paper Plus Decoupage Finish)

Glue Dots International
(262) 814-8500
www.gluedots.com

Provo Craft
(801) 794-9000
www.provocraft.com
(Terrifically Tacky Tape)

Images

Art Chix Studio
www.artchixstudio.com

Miscellaneous

JudiKins
(310) 525-1115
www.judikins.com
(Transparent Laminating Sheets)

CREDITS

We would like to thank Nicole Steiman and Rachel Williams of the ARTbar for coordinating the tag contest for this book. The ARTbar is a rubber stamping studio/store that rents time at their "bar" to anyone wanting to try their hand at paper arts. At the ARTbar everyone is an artist. Besides offering space, the use of their huge variety of stamps, and every paper and supply you can think of, the ARTbar offers classes, workshops and demonstrations.

The ARTbar
207 N. Broadway B6
Santa Ana, CA 92701
www.theartbar.net

We'd also like to thank the many paper artists who entered their tags for this contest.

Grateful acknowledgement is made to Kim Latham of Delta Technical Coatings for her support and cooperation.

Banar Designs Principals:
Barbara Finwall and Nancy Javier
Art Direction: Barbara Finwall
Editorial Direction: Nancy Javier

Photography: Stephen Whalen
Computer Graphic Design: Mark Aron
Project Direction: Jerilyn Clements
Additional designs by: Jerilyn Clements, Nancy Javier and Barbara Finwall

---

Published by

the art of everyday living®
LEISURE ARTS
5701 Ranch Drive
Little Rock, AR 72223
© 2004 by Leisure Arts, Inc.

Produced by

BANAR DESIGNS
P.O. Box 483
Fallbrook, CA 92088
banar@adelphia.net

All rights reserved. This publication is protected under federal copyright laws. Reproduction or distribution of this publication or any other Leisure Arts publication, including publications which are out of print, is prohibited unless specifically authorized. This includes, but is not limited to, any form of reproduction or distribution on or through the Internet, including posting, scanning, or e-mail transmission.

The information in this publication is presented in good faith, but no warranty is given, nor results guaranteed. Since we have no control over physical conditions surrounding the application of information herein contained, Leisure Arts, Inc. disclaims any liability for untoward results.